SIX-FIGURE BLOGGING BLUEPRINT:

HOW TO START AN AMAZINGLY PROFITABLE BLOG IN THE NEXT 60 DAYS (EVEN IF YOU HAVE NO EXPERIENCE)

By

Raza Imam

www.PassiveIncomePlaybook.com

Table of Contents

Need Help?

I've given you all the steps you need to get started, but if you ever need help, feel free to email me at raza@passiveincomeplaybook.com so my team and I can help.

Short and Sweet (Because We're All Busy)

"Give me a one-page bullet-list of exactly what I should do. That's

worth more to me than a stack of books that I have to dig through to

get to the good stuff. I may give you 50 bucks for the books. But I'll pay

you $5,000 for the one page."

-Alwyn Cosgrove, fitness coach, trainer, entrepreneur

You're busy.

I'm busy.

We're all busy.

It's an epidemic of the modern age.

That's why I kept this book short and sweet.

It's practical, it's tactical, and it's actionable.

Why?

Because I want to give you the meat and potatoes so that you can get started and take things to the next level - as soon as possible.

Because if you're like me, time is your most valuable asset.

Honestly, who actually has time to read 200-300 page books? With 3 young kids that need my attention, I sure don't!

It's also why CEO's have executive summaries prepared for them. Rather than spending hours and hours pouring over detailed reports, they need the most valuable information, distilled into actionable insights, so that they can make critical decisions and take action.

That's what I want for you.

You'll notice that there's a lot that I ***don't*** talk about in this book; that's for a reason.

My goal is to give you the quickest, easiest, simplest way to find leads and make sales on your blog.

Please note, I write in short, punchy paragraphs that are usually one or two sentences long. I do this because it makes it much easier for me to crank out ideas. When I write, I write from the heart and writing short paragraphs like this is a part of that.

I hope you enjoy reading this book as much as I enjoyed writing it.

Chapter 1

Suspend Your Disbelief

I know the claim of earning 6-figures from your blog is hard to believe.

But I want you to suspend your disbelief for a moment.

I know that making money with a blog will be met with some skepticism.

Things in the online money-making world move quickly (to say the least), so it is perfectly legitimate to wonder if blogging is still the money maker that it once was.

The answer is a **_resounding yes_**, provided that you know what you are doing.

Later in this book, I'm going to share real-life examples of people earning an amazing living by simply sharing their expertise with the world.

All through a humble blog.

"So how do they earn their money?"

Great question.

Consider this, many bloggers earn money through advertising, but that's just a drop in the bucket. For most bloggers, advertising earns just a few hundred dollars per month.

The classic method for making money on a blog is through ad revenue. A successful blog can bring in quite a bit of income through ads. For example, you can set up a PPC (pay-per-click) ad system wherein you get a small amount of revenue whenever someone clicks through to an ad. If you can get this to work, it can result in a tidy little amount of income.

However, ad revenue is a flawed method, to say the least. For starters, many people who browse blogs are internet savvy enough to either use ad blockers or to just straight up ignore ads (since they often get associated with things like viruses and scams).

So, ad revenue alone, even if you do get clicks, isn't going to be enough. Plus, the presence of ads does risk alienating many potential readers who may worry that the integrity of your writing is being compromised by advertisers.

So where does the rest of the income come from?

Well, it comes from a lot of different sources:

- **Online Courses**: This is my favorite way to make money from a blog. People have literally made millions of dollars selling online courses on topics as diverse as knitting, computer programming, putting babies to sleep, confidence, career change, public speaking, accounting, online advertising, and martial arts.

- **Coaching**: High-ticket coaching is a fantastic way to make money as well. Often times, people do coaching before creating an online course. When you consider how many people are willing to pay for an expert to coach them, it becomes easy to see why this is a fantastic way to make money.

- **Corporate Consulting**: If you blog about law, finance, accounting, marketing, or technology, your blog could provide a steady stream of high-paying corporate clients. Bloggers like Neil Patel, Chris Brogan, and others have earned millions of dollars by serving big corporations. And they got found via their blogs.

- **Speaking Engagements**: Similar to corporate consulting, some bloggers make big money by speaking to corporations, industry associations, and at conferences.

- **Selling Products**: Many bloggers write books, sell products like apparel or supplements, and even create mobile apps and sell TONS of units; all from their simple blog.

- **Sponsored Reviews of Products**: Some bloggers get paid by big companies to review their products. This is really popular with mobile phone blogs, toy blogs, camera blogs, and other tech blogs. In fact, I've seen a blog make money from reviewing baby strollers (my wife actually visited that blog to research a baby carrier and stroller set for one of our kids)

- **Affiliate Commissions**: Similar to the methods listed above, bloggers get paid by recommending other products and services. They don't get paid to advertise, but they do get a commission if a visitor clicks a link and buys the product.

Each of these products could account for thousands (*often times tens of thousands of dollars per month*)

When you think of it like that, you can start to see the potential.

Some people sell online courses that sell for $500-$1000.

Some people offer corporate training for $10,000 go $15,000 per engagement.

Some people promote credit cards and bank programs and earn up to $500 per sign up.

Some people earn affiliate commissions by promoting other people's ebooks and online courses.

Some people offer group coaching and charge $3,000 to $5,000 per client.

Imagine you start a blog about photography and sell an online course about photography for beginners. Or a niche course on camera lenses. Or a course on wildlife photography. *I've personally spent money on a photography course for my son.*

Or imagine you start a blog about sales performance and offer to train corporate sales teams. *I've personally bought a sales training course that I learned about via a blog.*

Or what if you're an expert on putting babies to sleep and offer coaching to help new parents that are struggling with parents. *My wife has personally bought a coaching package from a baby sleep coach.*

What if you write a blog about software development and people contact you to help them with projects? *I've personally gotten clients from a software blog I started earlier in my career.*

Or what if you created a blog that taught people how to play the piano or the guitar and then sold them online training courses? *This is a reality and dozens of people are making thousands, even tens of thousands of dollars selling courses.*

So rather than asking *"Is it even possible to make money from a blog?"* I want you to ask: *"What skills, talents, products, or services can I offer to people that solves a real problem that I can charge a premium price for?"*

Key Points:

So, to end this chapter, let's quickly review a few things.

- Blogs can _clearly_ still be used to make a significant income.

- But you **have** to write about something that people are interested in and are willing to pay money for.

- One thing that absolutely needs to be clear is that your blog won't make **any** money if there isn't an audience.

- You have to be credible, authentic, and honest.

- You need to have a monetization strategy.

All of the above strategies require you to have an audience (_it doesn't need to be huge_) to actually make you money. So, don't start fantasizing about your fortune just yet, you need to rest of this book and find out how to make a good blog that attracts your ideal readers and inspires them to buy from you.

We're going to cover some of that in the rest of this book.

Chapter 2

Low Costs, Huge Potential

This next chapter is meant to answer a very simple, but important question.

"Why would I ever want to start a blog?"

There are dozens, if not hundreds of ways to make a living online. Why would you want you ever want to start a blog when you can do one of these many other options?

There are a few reasons why a blog is a good way to make money online, but most importantly, you have to have a passion for whatever it is that you're writing about.

Low Startup Costs

Do you remember the old adage "it takes money to make money?" Well, that saying applies doubly so online. Most businesses require fairly sizeable investments in order for you to start making some serious money.

- I have a friend that spent $250,000 to open a restaurant... that eventually failed

- I know another guy that spent hundreds of thousands to open a laundromat

- My parents have invested HUGE amounts of money in their real estate business

- I know people that invested hundreds of thousands of dollars into a software business.

Now all of these businesses could make a lot of money, but they come with a **massive** upfront capital investment.

Blogs, when compared to many other activities, have nearly no startup costs.

Sure, there may be a fee to host your blog on a paid platform, but the $25 to $150 per month it costs to run a blog is _a drop in the bucket_ compared to starting a traditional brick-and-mortar business.

And if you monetize it right, the income potential could be **_astronomical_**.

If your blog doesn't catch on (and that is always a possibility, even if you do everything perfectly), then you haven't really lost much of anything.

Potential To Branch Out

In the last chapter, we discussed the multiple ways people are making money with their blogs.

Building a popular, well-respected blog is a great way to launch a thriving business.

You can *launch an online course*, *offer consulting*, *be invited* (and paid) *to speak to corporations*, *do live seminars*, and *publish books*.

All from a tiny little blog.

Even better, the credibility, connections, and expertise you gain from writing a blog can lead to an incredibly strong business in just a few years.

All with very little startup capital or investment (as long as you sell digital products like ebooks, online courses, or software)

It Generates Passive Income

One of the main reasons to go for a blog is because of the massive amount of passive income that it can generate.

I remember making my first ever sale online, it was incredible.

At the time I had a fitness blog about isometric and plyometric exercises. I was getting about 100 visitors to it per day.

I put enrolled for an affiliate program for a fitness product that paid a 60% commission for a $39.99 ebook if anyone clicked the link from my website and bought.

I remember getting the emails titled "cha-ching", informing me that I had made a commission of $24.95.

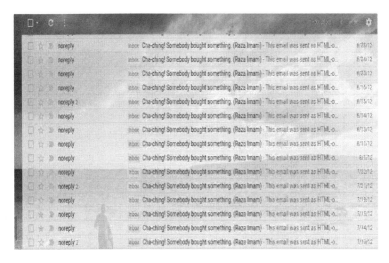

It was an incredible feeling.

I eventually went on to make $500 per month from this little blog, all because my readers clicked a link and bought a book that I didn't even write!

If you are marketing products or doing product reviews, then you can get a constant stream of sales from your blog. Sure, you will likely get a big rush when you first make your post. But, even after the initial rush is over you will still get a pretty steady stream of income from your blog posts.

You Can Work From Anywhere in the World

My parents own real estate. I have friends that own restaurants and retail stores.

I have a friend that owns a dental practice with his wife.

And they all make a good living.

But the common theme is that they have to be tied down to their business. They either have to provide the service, or manage employees, or otherwise be present at their business.

The beauty of starting an online business is that you can work from anywhere in the world. All you need is electricity, the ability to collect payments, and a reliable internet connection.

I know people that left the US to live in Costa Rica, Bali, India, Thailand, and Mexico and were able to live fun, thrilling lives based on the earnings from their online business.

Blogs Are Easy To Start

By far the best reason to start a blog is that it is extremely easy for anyone to do. One of the major barriers to any business is the large capital investment.

My parents had to invest millions of dollars into their real estate business.

My dentist friend had to invest $1 million dollars into each of his three offices. That includes building the place out and buying dental chairs, dental equipment, x-ray machines, televisions, etc.

I have a friend that lost $200,000 investing in a Middle Eastern restaurant in Miami.

I have another friend that's trying to start a software company. He needs $1 million dollars to hire more people and scale up his marketing efforts. He's been looking for investors for nearly 2 years and still hasn't found any.

So the barrier to entry is really low to start a blog.

You Don't Have to Be An "Expert"

Because the barrier to entry for starting a blog is so low, it's incredibly easy to start a blog. That means there are thousands of new blogs sprouting up.

But just because the barrier to entry is low for a blog doesn't mean that anyone can start a blog and make money.

If you want your blog to succeed, all you have to do is know how to write.

You have to have a passion for what you're writing about.

You have to be credible. You don't have to be a certified, credentialed, recognized "expert", but you do have to be credible. That means you have to be a real, authentic person that's sharing your experiences, failures, breakthroughs, and stories in a way that authentically connects with people.

Key Points:

So, to end this chapter, let's quickly review a few things.

- Blogs have low startup costs

- You don't have to be an expert

- You can gain lots of credibility, connections, and exposure

As you can see from this chapter, there are a lot of reasons why blogging is worthwhile and why you personally should consider it over other possible methods for making money online.

Chapter 3

Write About These Topics
(The Secret To A Wildly Successful Blog)

In this chapter, I reveal some great topics to start a blog about.

But before I reveal the best topics, I want you to keep one thing in mind - as long as you're solving people's problems, you'll never run out of an audience.

I want you to think about that for a second.

Because even though I don't personally know you, I think you have the potential to create an amazing blog.

Doubt me?

Well, consider this...

Starting a popular blog isn't as hard as you might think.

And if you've been alive for longer than 15 years, you probably have enough expertise in *something* to show others how to do it.

Sure, it takes consistent, passionate work and a willingness to promote your content, and I'll go into examples below, but consider this.

Most people that make a living from their blogs write about solving some kind of problem or helping people get to some kind of desired state.

The classic adage is that if you talk about health, wealth, or relationships, you'll never go broke.

That's why diet and weight loss books, magazines, pills, potions, gadgets, surgeries, and articles sell so well.

To the tune of billions of dollars per year.

Because people have a visceral desire to look and feel better.

It's the same reason why people that write about real estate investing, investing stocks, social media marketing, SEO, sales, how to create business plans, etc. do so well.

They are teaching people how to make more money and become more wealthy.

And that stuff sells.

21

So like I said, you ARE an expert in something.

And if you can spin your expertise and link it to health, wealth, or relationships, you're golden.

I'll show you what I mean later in this chapter.

Keep in mind, you don't need to be a "professional".

For example, I'm not a bodybuilder, or a certified personal trainer, or a health coach.

But I did write a bestselling fitness book.

Why?

Because I'm a normal guy and I was still able to get in shape despite a busy job, a growing family, and a long daily commute.

Rather than being viewed as an "impostor", I was viewed as someone who was able to "figure it out".

And if you look at the reviews from my book and blog *"The Science of Getting Ripped"*, you'll see that it's helped a lot of people.

So stop thinking you're an impostor, or a fake, or not worthy to write.

Because if you've solved a specific problem, then you ARE qualified to write.

And people will be willing to pay you to learn how you did it.

So be sure to include your personal story, your struggles, your breakthroughs and your "aha" moments.

Share the resources you used to achieve your goal and get the results you got.

Because THAT'S what people want to know.

Like the popular phrase goes *"facts tell, stories sell"*.

But as far as you being an expert, think about the following list of topics because I'm sure you know quite a bit about at least ONE of these topics.

Remember, you don't need to be an "expert".

You DO need to either have real-life experience solving a real problem that people face OR you should interview experts that have done something and compile *their* stories and put it into a blog.

That's what an unknown author named Napolean Hill did in 1937 when he wrote his perennial bestseller.

He interviewed the multi-millionaire businessmen of his time and distilled their advice into easy to digest points and called it "*Think and Grow Rich*".

As you may know, the book has been a bestseller for the past 81 years.

So the key is to focus on a problem or question that your potential readers could have, and to solve that problem or answer that question in the form of a blog, either with your own experience, or with someone else's.

Better yet, come up with a list of the top 20 questions that people in your industry have, and write a long, detailed blog post explaining how to solve it.

But remember, it has to be a real problem that people care about and are willing to spend money on.

If you don't solve a real need, then you likely won't make much income.

If you're already in a high-skilled field like real estate, law, medicine, accounting, computer programming, project management, human resources, copywriting, public speaking, finance, architecture, sales, human resources, organizational change, online marketing, social media expert, or any other highly skilled field, you're GOLDEN.

If you write about hobbies like skiing, snowboarding, horseback riding, chess, woodworking, sports cars, knitting, scrapbooking, cooking, interior design, painting, gaming, cell phones, or gardening - you're also GOLDEN.

If you write about personal issues like intimacy, depression, anxiety, self-confidence, meditation, mindfulness, productivity, or relationships, you're also GOLDEN.

Why?

Because those are all topics that people **_care_** about.

If you can solve people's problems, and tell them stories, share your experiences, talk about how you overcame your struggles - you'll build a bond and rapport with them that will cause them to like and trust you.

But what if you don't have a professional background?

No problem.

Bestselling author Hal Elrod wrote a book called "*The Miracle Morning Routine*" after getting in a car accident.

And he's built a multi-million dollar business from it.

Amazing, right?

So you don't need to be an expert in a profession.

You just need to have a great story to tell that solves a problem.

Here are a few popular examples:

- **House training a puppy**: Puppies are often bought on a whim. Someone is walking by a pet store, or sees an ad from a breeder, and suddenly they just have to have the cute little puppy. This often leads to people having pets that they are not ready to care for properly. These people get frazzled very easily and tend to go looking for house training tips and strategies online. Now, I know what you are thinking, "I can't write a blog about house training a puppy. I'm not a professional dog trainer." But the truth is that if you've successfully trained a dog before, or better yet, grew up around dogs, then you can write a very good blog post about house training a puppy. Personal experience counts for a lot. Your readers want to know about your struggles of coming home to a mess on the carpet. They want to hear how you solved that problem if you recommend a certain training strategy or tip, then follow it up with a quick story about what happened when you tried it on your own dog.

- **Getting in Shape**: Everyone wants to get in shape at some point in their life. Sure, there are popular weight loss programs and fitness routines, but do you know why they sell? Because of the results they achieve. In other words, the before and after transformation pictures is what convinces people to buy those programs. So if you've gotten in shape, and you have before and after pics, you can simply create a blog documenting how you did it, what you ate, how long it took, and what you felt during the process. And believe me, people will buy it because you're a real person just like them.

- **How to Put a Baby to Sleep**: When we had our first child, getting him to go and stay asleep was so hard. We expected that in the beginning. But not six months into it. So out of desperation, my wife bought 3 books on Amazon about putting a baby to sleep. She read about the different methods and philosophies. She even hired a baby sleep consultant after reading one of her books that she bought from Amazon. We now have 3 kids so my wife has a ton of experience. I joke that if my wife wanted to, she could start a blog on the subject - and people would eagerly read it.

- **Solving a Specific Health Issue** (acne, back pain, etc.): I used to have weird shoulder pain due to a weight lifting injury. So I started looking for remedies on YouTube and Google. Luckily it was a minor issue and the advice I learned in a few YouTube videos solved the problem, but I've read blog posts as well. To be clear, I'm not talking about writing a guide on how to cure cancer or deal with life-threatening injuries; but rather health issues like acne, back pain, neck pain, stuffy noses, etc. Health issues like that can usually be managed through home remedies, and thus many people do not go to the doctor for them. This is where your blog comes in. Lots of people have solutions or tips for dealing with managing chronic pains, bad cases of acne, and clogged nasal passages (just to name a few health issues); usually because they themselves have dealt with these issues before. So, if you have some home remedies, passed down through your family for generations, that helps deal with acne, then you can compile them into a blog. You can include strategies for reducing acne and managing acne in addition to your own home remedies. The same goes for chronic pain; everyone has their own stretches, exercises, etc., that they use to help remedy chronic back and neck pain; someone who is currently suffering from chronic pain would most likely go to Google and read blog posts and articles about it.

- **Using a Specific Social Media Platform to Grow Your Business**: Now here's a real money maker, especially if you sell to the right audience. Imagine you're a small business person with a struggling floral shop. You've tried different ways to advertise and none of them has really worked for you. You know about Instagram, and Facebook, and Twitter, and Snapchat, but you don't know how to use them to promote your business. What if someone wrote a blog post showing you exactly how to use those platforms to grow your business. What if they included screenshots, and detailed explanations, and results of other businesses like you that used these platforms to grow their business. Wouldn't you read it? Of course you would! And people ARE making money writing about using LinkedIn, Facebook, Instagram, and SnapChat, so if you know how to use these platforms to grow a business, you can too.

- **Dealing with Stress**: Chronic stress is a public health issue. It is the root cause of so many diseases and disorders that there is a billion dollar industry around stress relief, from books to expensive seminars. If you've discovered how to conquer stress and tension in your life, then people want to know. It's even better if you have a high-stress life like being a busy parent, or a business owner, or a corporate executive, or a grief counselor. Your advice will ring true because of your background and struggles. If you have personal experience dealing with stress and have developed a unique way of dealing with it, then compile your expertise into a popular blog.

- **Creating a Business Plan That Generates Money**: It may sound odd, but you would be surprised by the number of people who rush into a business without having a clear, concise idea of what they want their business to accomplish in the next few years. If you have experience running or creating a small business, then you can create a very popular blog detailing how to create a clear business plan. Have you started a floral shop? Are you a dentist that has grown your practice? Are you a marketing expert that has shown small businesses how to grow? If so, document it.

- **Photography Tips**: If you have ever bought a camera for someone as a present before, then you know that buying someone a quality camera almost instantly turns them into an amateur photographer for a couple of weeks. Most people eventually settle down and only use the camera for special occasions, but some others develop an actual passion for photography. My former boss was obsessed with his camera, always reading about it, researching it, and taking photos during his family vacation. If you're like him, you could easily start a blog about photography for beginners. Since

31

schooling or workshops hosted by professionals can be expensive, would be amateur photographers will often search online for helpful blogs. A quality blog written by someone with experience in amateur photography can focus on a wide array of topics; including what accessories to get, how to properly photograph landscapes and people, how to set up a shot, the topics are endless.

- **Wedding Planning**: Expecting parents are some of the most stressed people in the world, but brides and grooms-to-be aren't far behind. I know I was stressed when I planned my wedding! Since most people do not know the first thing about wedding planning, they will inevitably turn to the internet for information, inspiration, and ideas. If you have experience planning weddings, then making a clear, easy to follow blog detailing how to properly plan for a wedding (as well as detailing tips and tricks for how to get the best deals, save money, etc.) would be a great idea. Not only will it sell well, but because people are always getting married, you'll never have to worry that your book becoming obsolete.

- **How to Better at Public Speaking**: Not everyone is born to speak to crowds, but unfortunately for those people, giving speeches to an audience is a talent that is quite helpful in many different business sectors. Given how important public speaking is, many people will turn to the internet to learn how to do it properly. If you consider yourself a natural speaker, or you overcame poor public speaking skills, then you have the ability to run a high-quality blog geared toward people that want to speak. Give people exercises that they can do to improve their speaking skills, give them tips to help get their nerves under control while speaking, etc.

- **Mentoring Troubled Youth**: I recently heard that "school refusal" is becoming a thing with teenagers. They aren't quite dropping out, but they're refusing to go to school due to a variety of reasons (bullying, anxiety, substance abuse, etc.) Then there's the issue of kids with domestic problems that affect their performance and behavior in school. Lastly, there's the issue of kids that just don't apply themselves academically. Mentoring troubled youth probably has some of the greatest social impact on society. Mentoring troubled youth, putting them on the right path, and actually connecting with them is a very high-yield activity for society. And any stories, techniques, or results you can share would likely do very well. Just imagine starting a blog on how to prevent bullying, a little blog you create could turn into major media coverage if the book really produces results, or shares your "in the trenches" story of how you solved it at your school.

- **Building Money-Making Websites**: Remember how I talked about social media blogs and how they can be useful for businesses and marketers who need to use social media, but don't know how? Well, the same principle applies to building websites. Plenty of small business owners and internet marketers need to create websites. Often times the technical part isn't hard, it's the messaging. Writing the copy. Creating "words that sell". That speak to a certain market. That address a major problem. That promise an end result. So even if you aren't technical, if you know how to write, you can

STILL show people how to make money with their website.

- **Selling Products Online:** There are a LOT of people making a full-time income selling products on eBay, Amazon, Craigslist, etc. For others, it's a nice source of income on the side. Either way, more and more people are starting to experiment with selling products online. Because of that, online courses and blogs detailing how to get into selling online are very popular. It is not surprising, the process may seem simple, but actually getting into selling online is very complicated. You have to know the rules of the site you are selling on, you have to know what type of products sell best, and you have to know where to get products at cheap prices. If you have ever sold products online successfully, then compiling your experiences and knowledge into a popular blog is really a no brainer. There are always new people getting into online retail for the first time, and they are always looking for guides, courses, and blogs to help them out.

- **Saving Money and Personal Finance**: Not everyone is great when it comes to managing their money. Some people cannot seem to live within their means, and spend money like it never runs out. If you have any tips or strategies for saving money and budgeting properly, that's the birth of a great blog. You don't even need to say anything new or novel. You can simply share your experiences with using the "envelope system" like Dave Ramsey talks about. Or you could write about how you went for 6 months without eating out. Or how you got out of debt in 12 months by selling unwanted stuff in your house. I know people that have done stuff like that and their stories are really, really interesting. If they compiled it into a book I'd definitely want to buy it.

- **Grooming/Beauty/Personal Care**: Do you know about men's grooming? Or looking good in your 40's? Or do you have an eclectic sense of style by shopping solely at thrift stores? If so, I'm willing to bet that people will pay for it. Looking good and being accepted are basic human emotions, and if you tap into that, you can start to build a very nice passive income. You don't have to work at a beauty salon or be a professional stylist to start a blog about personal grooming. If you feel you have a good sense of style, or your friends and family are constantly complimenting your grooming, then you can write a quality book about the topic.

- **Travel Advice**: Let's say you were (or currently are) a backpacker, traveling around the world, staying in hostels and Airbnbs in exotic countries. What if you finance your travels from credit card airline points? Don't you think people would want to know about that? What if you compiled a list of the best hotels, best credit cards, and best restaurants you've discovered in your years of traveling. Wouldn't people want to read that? Or let's say you're a corporate road warrior, traveling 5 days a week and you've figured out how to stay in shape while on the road. Don't you think people similar to you would want to know that knowledge?

This list barely scratches the surface of what you could write about.

But you can probably see that the most popular topics address a core human emotion.

Whether that's the emotion to make more money.

Or the emotion to be liked and loved and desired by other people.

Or the emotion of being freedom and peace of mind.

You already ARE an expert in something.

Even if you don't think you are, your life experiences and unique perspective gives you credibility.

Your job is to figure out how to link your expertise to a basic emotion.

I can't stress that enough.

So if you can tie your topic into health, wealth, or relationships, you'll be golden.

So if you write about gardening, you could write about how to create a stunning backyard that boosts your property value by $25,000.

Or if you write a cookbook, you can focus on how your recipes save money, or help lose weight, or can save a busy family precious time because they're so quick and easy to cook.

Or what if you're a swim instructor and have built a side business teaching kids how to swim on the weekends. You could start a blog showing how you've helped mentor kids through swimming, and share the life lessons you've learned. Or you could explain how you've built a profitable side hustle by teaching kids how to swim.

So spend some time thinking about what you're good at and what you want to share.

Because as long as you know how to relate that to core human emotions and desires, you can make a very sustainable passive income.

The main difficulty of picking a niche comes from the fact that you have to balance two competing factors.

On the one hand, you want to write about something that you are both passionate about and that you know about.

On the other hand, you also have to write about something that a large group of people will be interested in and that can be monetized in some way (obviously, if you are blogging as a hobby, this last part doesn't apply but most of you probably aren't blogging hobbyists).

Don't Decide Solely Based On Monetization Potential

After reading that previous section, you may be wondering to yourself "should I just pick the most profitable niche that I can find?"

The answer to this is no and there is a good reason for this. If you just pick a niche based on its money-making ability it is going to reflect in your posts.

People are smart enough to recognize when someone has no idea what they're talking about. A blog is only as good as the content in it. In order to produce good, informative content you need to have at least some interest and familiarity in a topic.

A popular route is to take the "curious novice" approach where you document your journey to learning something.

So, do some serious thinking. Think about topics that could potentially be profitable and that you have some interest and/or knowledge in. You don't have to be a world-renowned expert on the topic, but you should have some baseline knowledge and at least a passing interest in it.

I'm Still Struggling To Figure Out a Niche, What Should I Do?

If you are still struggling to come up with a niche (*and that isn't an uncommon problem, so don't worry if you are*), there are some strategies that you can try that might help you.

Sit down with a pen and paper and start writing down things that you are good at and that you do for fun.

Once you have about 5 or 6 entries under each category, go through each one and ask yourself "is there anything connecting these things together?"

For example, if you notice that a lot of things on your lists involve computers, then you may want to consider that as a potential niche.

How To Tell If There Is An Audience For Your Niche

With certain niches, it's pretty obvious if there is an audience or not.

There is always going to be an audience for things like online marketing, cooking, fashion, etc. So, if your niche falls into one of those broad categories, don't worry about it.

However, if you aren't sure about whether there is an audience for your niche, you can always check for other popular blogs. If there are, then you've got a hot niche - and a list of potential partners (*more on that in a later chapter*)

The Concept of Evergreen Content

Evergreen topics are topics that will remain popular, meaning they will always be in demand.

Things like relationship advice, investing, parenting, stress relief, business, technology, fitness, fashion, etc. will always be in demand. There will always be new developments, new trends, new technology, new breakthroughs, so there will never be a shortage of things to write about.

Key Points:

So, to end this chapter, let's quickly review a few things.

- You **don't** need to be an "*expert*" in something - you just need to have an interest in it

- There are tons of things you can write about, focus on problems your audience is having and share stories about how to solve them

- Write about things that people are truly interested in that have profit potential - not sure if there's potential? Just look for other popular blogs on the topic.

Now that you've chosen a topic, let's start talking about how to set up your blog. That's what the next chapter is about.

Chapter 4

Getting Setup The Easy Way (Step-By-Step) Technical Stuff - Hosting, Domain Names, And Content Management System

Now that you know both how to make money with a blog and why you want to start a blog in the first place, it is time to move onto the real reason most of you are reading this, which is for a guide on how to set up your own blog.

This chapter will give you a high-level overview of how to set up a blog technically, and I include simple, step-by-step instructions (with pictures) that show you how to setup up a blog in just a few minutes.

But before we begin, let's start with some definitions and why they're important:

- **Domain Names**: A domain name is the website address for your blog. Just like Google.com or Amazon.com or CNN.com. So you'll want to think of a memorable, catchy, and unique domain name before you start your blog

- **Web Hosting**: Rather than you buying a server of your own, web hosting companies host your website for you. That means they manage the technical aspect of your website so that you can focus on writing and promoting content. They typically host hundreds of thousands, if not millions of other websites, so they're very secure and have the infrastructure in place to make websites fast, secure, and reliable.

- **Content Management System**: These days, very few people create websites from scratch. Rather than code a website, they use a content management system. (CMS). Think of a CMS as a framework to write, it's almost like a word processor for your website.

In this chapter, I'm going to give you my top recommendations for buying domain names, where to get web hosting, and my absolute favorite content management system.

My goal in this chapter is to simplify this stuff for you so that you can get started creating your blog right away.

Choosing a Domain Name

As for a domain name, I strongly recommend that you choose something that accurately describes your business, your personality, or both.

Focus on being unique, distinct, creative, and authentic so that your audience resonates with it. The more memorable, impactful, and compelling the better.

For example, here are some great domain names of very popular blogs:

CopyBlogger.com - A blog about copywriting

SmartPassiveIncome.com: A blog about earning passive income online

LifeHacker.com: A mega-popular blog that shares life hacks

TechCrunch: A blog about Silicon Valley startups

TreeHugger.com: An environmental blog

TheConsumerist.com: A blog about protecting consumer rights in an age of corporatism

SearchEngineLand.com: A blog about search engine optimization and marketing

FitnessBlackBook.com: A fitness blog created by a guy that used to be a suit salesman

NerdFitness.com: Another fitness blog created by a regular guy that appealed to a very specific audience (this blog is HUGELY popular now)

Fluentin3Months.com: A language learning blog that shows you how to become fluent in 3 months (I love this idea)

Now, these are examples of _incredibly_ popular blogs, but hopefully, you understand what I mean about creating a memorable, brandable domain name that sticks out in your target audience's mind.

So for this part, I want you to think of a domain name for your blog.

Remember, you want this blog to represent your business and your unique approach to your industry, so don't skimp here.

My best piece of advice is to list out 20+ names for your blog. It sounds like a lot, but this is a key piece of advice that the world's best copywriters and ad experts use to brainstorm amazing ideas - I use it regularly and strongly suggest that you do the same.

Your blog has to catch a new reader's attention in 5 seconds, so it's worth 30 minutes thinking of a good domain name.

As for me, I've created lots of blogs, but here are my most popular domain names:

TheScienceofGettingRipped.com: This is my fitness website

5XYourFocus.com: This is my personal development website

PassiveIncomePlaybook.com: This is my passive income website

As you can see, I worked hard to make sure that they are memorable and unique.

You want to do the same thing.

A domain name should cost you between $5 to $20 dollars.

Of course, some domain names can cost thousands, tens of thousands, hundreds of thousands, and even millions of dollars depending on how popular the term is - but you won't be buying a domain like that.

Because in all honesty, the most popular ones are already taken.

Often times, people buy popular or catchy sounding domain names and then auction them off for thousands of dollars.

For example, people got filthy rich buying domain names and then selling them to big companies. Just take a look at this list…

CarInsurance.com: $47 million

Insurance.com: $35.6 million

PrivateJet.com: $30.18 million

VacationRentals.com: $35 million

Internet.com: $30 million

Insure.com: $16 million

Clearly, those domain names are in hot finance, investing, and luxury travel industries, but it gives you an idea of what companies are willing to spend for a brandable domain name.

I **don't** recommend buying anything similar. Instead, I recommend creating something memorable, unique, and authentic that your audience will identify with.

7 Things to Look for in a Domain and Web Hosting Company

Before I reveal my #1 recommendation for buying domain names and setting up web hosting, I want to let you know the top 10 things you should be looking for.

1). Reliability: A good web hosting company should be able to guarantee 99.9% uptime. That means the server should be safe, secure, and operational 99.9% of the time. Most hosting companies guarantee this and have contingency plans if their servers go down.

2). Affordability: A basic web hosting plan should cost no more than $20 per month, often times much less, especially if you're a beginner. The price will go up depending on additional features you add like extra security, email hosting, application hosting, etc. But for most bloggers, that's not relevant.

3). Customer Support: This is a big one. Your web hosting company should offer 24/7 customer support via phone and chat to help you if your site goes down, you need help installing something, or you have a general question. Most professional web hosting companies offer stellar, world-class customer support - because they understand how important it is.

4). One-Click Installs: This is another incredibly important feature. You want to be able to install your content management system (CMS) quickly and easily. Remember, you're a blogger, not a developer or programmer, so being able to quickly install your blogging platform on your hosting server is really important. Most hosting companies offer one-click installs of the most popular CMS's like Wordpress, Drupal, Joomla, etc.

5). Free Security: Your hosting company should include a free Secure Socket Layer (SSL) certificate that provides security for your website by encrypting communications between the server and visitors to your website. It will flag your site secure by displaying a padlock icon in your address

51

bar so that hackers can't hack the traffic between your website and your reader's computers

6). Unlimited Storage and Bandwidth: Your web hosting company should offer you unlimited storage and bandwidth. That means that you won't be charged if you have a lot of images, videos, and pages on your blog - you also won't be charged based on how many visitors come to your blog.

7). Free Backups: Your hosting company should be automatically backing up your site, so in the event that your site gets hacked, or the server crashes, they can bring it back up quickly and easily.

My #1 Pick for Domain Names and Web Hosting

Picking where to host your blog is like picking where to build a house. You have to pick solid land that gives you the ability to expand your house as more people live there.

The same concept applies to your domain name and where you host your blog.

As for buying domain names and web hosting, my absolute favorite is HostGator.com

Why?

I've been using them for years, since 2009 actually, and they have some of the best customer service in the business.

They're affordable, extremely reliable, have phenomenal customer support, and the one that I'm most familiar with.

Here's a chart that shows how they compare against other popular options:

Features	GoDaddy Economy Hosting Plan	HostGator Hatchling Plan	Squarespace Personal Plan
Starting Monthly Price On Introductory Offer	$2.99	$2.75	$12.00
Monthly Renewal Cost	$7.99	$6.95	$12.00 - $16.00
Domains	1	1	1
Pages	Unlimited	Unlimited	Unlimited
Storage	100 GB	Unmetered	Unlimited
Bandwidth	Unmetered	Unmetered	Unlimited
Free Email Addresses	1	Unlimited	0
$100 Google Adwords		✓	

As you can see, they're cheaper and have more features than the other companies.

That's why I've used HostGator for years, highly recommend them - *and will continue to do so.*

I've even got a deal for my readers where you can get your domain name and web hosting for as little as $3 per month.

Click here to check it out.

To be clear, they'll charge you up front, but you save almost 75% on the total cost, which is an incredible deal.

How to Get Setup with HostGator

As for buying a domain name and hosting, it's a really simple process, and below are simple screenshots that walk you through it.

1) . **Click here** (or jaggededgedigital.com/hostgator-deal) to get the $3/month deal

2) . Click the "**Get Started Now**" button

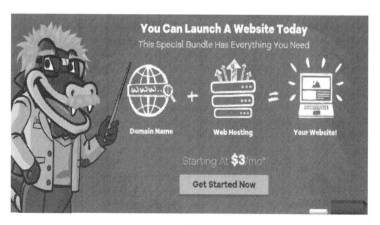

3) Search for a domain name that you want in the "**Enter Your Domain**" box.

Remember the list of names you came up with earlier. If it's available, buy the ".com" version. In this case, I searched for the domain "ILove90sFashion.com" (*don't judge*) and it's available for $5/year.

4) Then go to the "**Choose Your Hosting Plan**" section and choose the hosting plan you want:

2. Choose a Hosting Plan

5) After that, go to the "**Enter Your Billing Info**" section and fill that out.

3. Enter Your Billing Info

6) Then go to "**Review Your Order Details**" and check out.

Why Wordpress? (the world's most popular CMS)

Now that you've bought your domain name and have your web hosting setup, you have a lot of CMS's that you can use.

And your web hosting company will provide them to you free of charge.

The most popular are Wordpress, Joomla, Drupal, and Magento.

But one of them is the hands-down best in my opinion.

There are dozens of content management systems on the market, and most of them are quite good, but the #1, most popular, most versatile one is Wordpress.

I've been using Wordpress websites ever since 2009 and I'm in love with it.

Here's why:

1) **Used by Over 70 Million Websites**: Wordpress is the most popular CMS on the planet, running on over 70 million websites.

2) **Ease of Use**: Think of Wordpress as a word processor for the web. You can use it to create amazing blogs and websites, with no coding expertise or complicated technical setup. That's a big reason that's it's used on so many websites.

3) **Versatility**: From world-famous blogs to tiny niche websites, Wordpress meets the needs of a wide range of websites. It has hundreds of thousands of free plugins, widgets, themes, and tools that allow you to create custom contact forms, to dynamic sliders, to analytics code, to social media promotion. It's incredibly powerful, and another reason that so many websites use it.

4) **Gives You Full Control**: In addition to being extremely easy to use, Wordpress is extremely easy to customize and modify if you have the skills (or pay someone that does)

5) **Tons of Guides and Tutorial**: There are literally tens of thousands (if not hundreds of thousands) or articles, blog posts, videos, guides, and tutorials on how to set

up Wordpress. In fact, there are so many that you can literally solve any problem you run into by doing a quick Google search. And in the rare event that you can't, there are tons of forums, discussion boards, Reddit threads, and Facebook groups that you can turn to for help.

6) **Search Engine Optimization**: Finally, WordPress makes SEO (search engine optimization) very easy. That means it's already set up for search engines to find your site and index the content. This helps your website appear when users search for keywords and search terms on Google.

How to Install Wordpress

Setting up a Wordpress is incredibly easy. When I first learned, it took me just 30 minutes or so.

Below are step-by-step instructions on how to do that.

1) Log into your **Cpanel** by going to your websitename.com/cpanel and enter your username and password

2) In the "*Software*" section, click on the **QuickInstall** icon

3) On this page you'll click the **One-Click Installs** option:

4) Then select the **WordPress** icon

5) Using the drop-down menu chose the domain that WordPress should be installed to as well as any subdirectory you would like the site to load from if desired. **Example:** Should you wish your WordPress URL to be example.com/site instead of just example.com.

6) Complete the form with the following details:

1. For *Blog Title*, enter the name of the website. This is what will appear in the header as the name of your site.
2. For *Admin Username*, enter your preferred username.
3. Your first name.
4. Your last name.
5. For *Admin Email*, enter an email address where you want the admin password emailed to. Make sure this is a working email address.
6. Check the box next to the Terms of Service Agreement.
7. Click the orange **Install** button when you're ready to proceed.

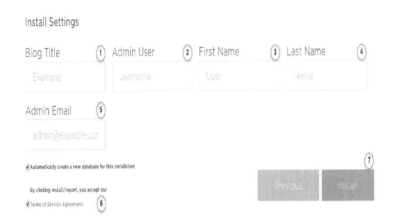

7) A progress bar will inform you of the progress of your installation. When complete, click **Details** for your admin URL, username, and password:

Now your Wordpress website should be all set up. In the next chapter, I'll show you how to design and style it so that you can get to the important part; writing blog posts and making money.

Key Takeaways:

- There are dozens of web hosting and domain registrar companies, but HostGator is my absolute favorite.

- There are lots of CMS's on the market, and most of them are free, but Wordpress is by far the most versatile and easiest to use of them all.

Lastly, don't forget to use my special HostGator discount link that gives you your domain name and web hosting at an insane 75% discount.

<u>Here's that link again...</u>

Chapter 5

Designing A Beautiful, Responsive Blog
(*Quickly And Easily*)

So, if you have been following this book step-by-step, you now have a niche, a hosting site, and a blog name picked out.

Now, it is time to move onto the next step, which is actually designing your blog (or getting it designed).

I won't go through the steps of designing your blog in this chapter because it's way too complicated to explain in an ebook. Plus, there are tons of tutorials on the subject online (I'll link to some of them at the end of this chapter).

However, I **will** show you my favorite tools to design your blog, what to include to make your blog stand out, and how to get more help if you need it.

Why Is Having A Well-Designed Blog So Important?

It's no exaggeration to say that *design* and *content* are the biggest factors to a blog's success. I'll be covering content later in this book, so for now, let's focus on design.

It is probably pretty obvious why having a well-designed blog is important, but for the sake of being complete, let's go over why it is so important. As has been mentioned before, there are thousands upon thousands of blogs out there all competing for readers' attention.

When a reader first comes to your blog, what is the first thing they will see? It won't be your content, it will be the overall design and look of your blog. So, if you don't have a good-looking blog, potential readers will never give it second look.

Think about it from a reader's perspective; if someone lands on a site that has no personality, doesn't take itself seriously, and makes no attempt at being clear, professional, and sleek, why would they ever trust you - let alone buy from you?

You literally have 3 seconds to make a good impression on a reader, **so you have to make it count.**

So it's **_vital_** that you focus not only on the content, but on the design.

A good-looking blog also builds authority. It may sound shallow, but we all judge a book by its cover. A sloppy, outdated, ugly blog screams laziness and carelessness - not qualities we want to be known for.

I mean, you wouldn't take financial advice from someone wearing a sloppy pair of sweatpants, would you?

8 Elements of Beautiful Blog Design:

Now "beautiful" design is a bit subjective, so I've identified the most important elements to incorporate into your blog design.

Don't worry if you don't feel overwhelmed by any of these because later in this chapter I reveal some great resources you can use to create gorgeous blogs.

1) Lots of White Space:

This is absolutely critical. The human eye is very complex, but it craves simplicity. A cluttered, ugly, busy site is a major turn off, so creating a blog with lots of white space and breaks between paragraphs is incredibly important.

Some of the web's most popular blogs even write in short 2-3 sentence paragraphs so that it's easier on readers' eyes. This is a subtle, but incredibly important feature of gorgeous design.

2)   Amazing Images:

Having beautiful images adds to the credibility of your blog. Having relevant images captures the reader's curiosity and accentuates the content.

There are tons of great websites that provide free, royalty-free images like Unsplash.com and Pixabay.com So there's no excuse not to add at least one image to your blog.

Ideally, you want to have multiple images, screenshots, and illustrations on your blog, but at the very least, you need to have a featured image for each blog post. Featured images are what show up on the homepage of your blog. They're literal "click-magnets" so be sure to include one in every post.

3)   Well-Written Headlines:

The world's best advertisers often spend 80% of their time on the headline of their content. Even fiction writers spend an immense amount of time on the opening line of their novel.

Why?

Because it's _that_ important.

Remember, you have 3 seconds to make an impression on your reader, so a clear, compelling, direct, benefit-laden headline is non-negotiable for every single blog post.

Good headlines should identify a problem, call out a specific audience, hint at a solution, give a timeframe, convey ease, and tell a story.

A tall order?

Absolutely.

The good news is that there are dozens of amazing guides and templates online that show you how to write great headlines.

4)   Scanability:

Since most high-quality blog posts should be 2000-5000 words, the ability to scroll down and scan a blog post is incredibly important.

The use of short paragraphs, sub-headings, bold, italicized text, and bullet points is critical to make the content easy to read and digest. Remember, most of your readers will be on mobile devices, so you want to make the content as easy to read as possible.

5)   Clear Navigation:

Imagine walking into a grocery store and not knowing where the produce section is, or the deli, or the bakery, or the dairy section. You'd likely walk out.

Brick and mortar stores understand the importance of clearly guiding the customer through the store - often times they hire psychologists to design the store so that the customer is lead down the path that will make them most likely to buy.

As I'm writing this book, I'm sitting at a Whole Foods Cafe and see signs saying "Fishmonger", "Butchershop", "Cafe", "Customer Service", "Health and Beauty", etc.

Having a clean, simple, easy to follow guide on where customers should go on your site is a tactic that the world's most popular blogs follow.

The most common links are:

- About Me

- Start Here

- Contact Me

- Blog

- Recommended Resources

- Top Posts

After your homepage, your "About Me" page is the most visited site on your entire blog, so you want to make it count.

Include pictures of yourself and pictures of anything that lends credibility to how you are and the results you provide.

Before and after pictures are powerful for fitness blogs. Earnings reports are powerful for finance blogs. Family pictures are powerful for relationship and parenting blogs.

So pay attention to these pages and be sure to include them in your navigation.

6) Recency:

A well-designed blog has to not only be relevant, but it also has to be _recent._

That means you have to regularly update your blog if you want readers to take you seriously. Your content has to be up to date and convey that you're actively involved.

Some bloggers will even update posts from years ago - that way they show that they're still recent and relevant without having to completely create new content.

7) Social Proof:

Social proof means that other people trust you. And if other people trust you, new readers will be more likely to trust you.

That's why you see big blogs include the following:

- Number of email subscribers

- Number of social media followers

- Awards, recognition, and accolades

- Media mentions

These are all incredibly important, and are prominently visible "above the fold" so that users don't have to scroll far.

The point is to make a strong impression on readers and show them that it's safe for them to trust you because thousands of other people do the same.

8) Personality:

Lastly, your blog has to be infused with personality.

Humans crave intimacy, authenticity, stories, imagery, and emotion - *and it's your job to give that to them.*

As a blogger, you're a real person, not some nameless, faceless corporation. You don't have a multi-million dollar marketing budget behind you. You don't have a horde of mediocre writers generating content to satisfy Google's algorithms.

You're a living, breathing human being that is sharing your story with other human beings - *and **that's** your secret weapon.*

Infusing personality, emotion, story, authenticity, and imagery in every post you write is what will set you apart,

71

create trust, and build a loyal following that not only follows you, but that trusts and buys from you.

Some of the most popular blogs on the planet understand this and work hard to infuse their personality on their blogs.

Examples Beautiful Blogs

Now that we've gone over the most important elements of a beautiful blog, let me show you a few examples of sites that are doing it right.

GrowthLab: This site is run by personal finance blogger and author Ramit Sethi. You'll notice the white space, beautiful images, great headlines, and clear writing. It's one of my favorite websites for a reason.

ReadWrite: This is a tech website focused on topics like artificial intelligence, startups, blockchain, and financial technology. They employ great images, concise headlines, and beautiful design.

MakingSenseofCents: This is a personal finance website that makes $100,000 per month (*you read that right*) sharing how she got out of debt. She includes lots of social proof and focuses her content on her story. One of her most powerful aspects is her story of getting out of debt and making money from her blog.

JayFerruggia: Jay Ferruggia is a fitness coach and author and has an amazing blog and podcast geared toward middle-aged men that want to be healthy, fit, and successful. Central to his blog is a minimalist design and content that speaks directly to his audience.

SmartBlogger: This is one of my favorite blogs in terms of both content and design. Jon Morrow literally does everything right from navigation, to social proof, to images, to headlines, readability. This is **_the_** blog to model in terms of design.

The Perfect Blog Platform (my absolute FAVORITE)

When it comes to designing a blog, you want to get to it as fast as possible without wasting time.

I don't want you getting bogged down in researching the dozens of options, struggling to learn how to use them, or wrestling with design issues.

My goal is to get you set up as quickly as possible so you can focus on what matters most; creating and promoting amazing content.

With that said, my *all-time favorite* blog platform is called ThriveThemes.

They are the most amazing, most cost-effective, most beautiful theme out there.

I can't speak highly enough about them.

Here's why...

It's Fast: ThriveThemes is built for speed, readability, and clarity. Their themes are packed with features that make your website building life easy.

Easy Email List Building: Their ThriveLeads plugin is your all-in-one email list building tool. It allows you to create and easily design every type of opt-in form, run A/B tests and grow your list faster than ever before.

Gorgeous Visual Editor: Forget having to code. ThriveThemes has the fastest and most intuitive visual editor for WordPress. Easily create drag-and-drop layouts, add buttons and advanced content elements and much more... I use it all time time.

Awesome Widgets: ThriveThemes allows you to display different content in your widget areas, based on posts, pages, categories, tags, and advanced targeting rules.

Makes Testing Super Simple: Remember how important headlines are? Well, ThriveThemes has a tool that allows you to test different headlines against each other. For each blog post, Thrive Headline Optimizer will A/B test your titles and show only the highest performing ones.

Easily Build Scarcity: It's no secret that scarcity sells. That's why limited time offers do so well. ThriveThemes has the perfect scarcity marketing tool for WordPress. It allows you to increase your conversions by adding countdown timers, run complex evergreen scarcity campaigns and much more.

Lively Comments Section: Part of social proof means you need to have a lively comments section on each blog post. The more comments you have, the more likely readers are to view you with trust and authority. ThriveThemes helps you increase engagement through several innovative features like upvoting and downvoting, gamified comment incentives and an impressive number of after-comment-actions.

These are just a few features that make ThriveThemes so awesome - and as I said, they're my absolute favorite Wordpress theme.

Still not convinced?

Check out these awesome case studies of people that have used ThriveThemes to create amazing blogs that earn them money.

Interested?

Click here to get special pricing on ThriveThemes.

Essential (mostly free) WordPress Plugins

ThriveThemes gives you almost everything you need to launch a fast, responsive, beautiful blog.

Since you'll be using WordPress as, you should take advantage of the amazing plugins let you add all sorts of features like SEO (search engine optimization, email marketing, contact forms, site analytics, and making your website faster.

But there are also a few free plugins that I strongly suggest that you install.

1)   Yoast SEO

This plugin makes it easier for Google to crawl your site and appear in the search engine results pages. It helps you improve your blog titles, descriptions, images and content length so that more people find your blog on Google.

There are other plugins that do the same, but this is the most popular one by far.

2)   WPForms

This plugin makes it easy to create contact forms so that people can easily contact you.

3)   Sumo

Sumoe has incredibly popular plugins that make it easy to create social share buttons, email captures, and more. Most of their plugins are free so I highly recommend that you use them.

4)   LuckyOrange

This is an awesome analytics plugin that shows not only where your users come from, but it also shows what they do on your site, where they click, and how far they scroll down. It's an amazing plugin at an incredible price.

5) BackupBuddy

This plugin allows you to quickly and easily backup your blog just in case it crashes.

6) W3 Total Cache

Google has stated that the faster a website loads, the more likely it is to rank highly when a user enters a search term - so you want to take site speed seriously. W3 Total Cache reduces the size of files on your blog so it loads faster when people land on it.

7) MaxCDN

This is another plugin that improves the speed and responsiveness of your site. It's an absolute must-have.

Should You Design the Blog Yourself Or Hire A Professional

I've covered a lot in this chapter, so the last thing I want to discuss is whether you should design the blog yourself or hire a professional.

Remember, my goal is for you to get started as quickly as possible. I want you to get to the *fun* and *profitable* part which is writing and promoting content that your audience loves.

So, when it comes to designing a nice looking blog, you have two choices, you can either do it yourself or you can hire one of the many freelancers out there to do it for you.

There's no correct option as both methods have pros and cons. However, for most of you reading this, the best option will likely be to use a freelancer for reasons that are going to be explored.

Doing It Yourself

Now, you are probably saying to yourself "I can't design the blog myself, I don't have any experience with web design."

There are so many tutorials online, if you are willing to put in the effort, you can design your own blog fairly easily.

This is what I've done myself for every one of my blogs.

And if you use tools like ThriveThemes, this is incredibly easy to do.

Of course, you'll save time, and build valuable skills that you can offer as a service in the future as well.

Lastly, designing the blog yourself also enables you to make on the fly adjustments or upgrades whenever you want. Your blog will likely change as it grows, so having this skill allows you to make changes whenever you want.

Hiring A Freelancer

As far as hiring a professional, if you know you'll struggle with the technical aspects of setting up your blog, it makes sense to hire someone.

Fighting with the technology, making mistakes, and struggling to make the design just right is exhausting - and wastes valuable time.

Trust me, I've been there.

I've spent an entire week learning how to set up and design my blogs before, and now that I think about it, I could have used that time to write and promote content instead.

You need to look at your blog like a business and yourself as the CEO. Focus on CEO tasks and outsource the rest.

Often times, you can find freelancers that know how to customize and optimize themes and plugins - so it's not like you'll be spending tons of money.

So my best advice is to use something like ThriveThemes and hire a freelancer that has experience with it to tweak it.

It's the best of both worlds really.

Key TakeAways

As I end this chapter, I want to leave you with a few takeaways.

Ultimately the decision on whether to do your blog yourself or to hire someone is entirely up to you. Regardless of what decision you end up making, there are some things to keep in mind.

- **Mobile Friendly**: Being mobile friendly is **not** optional. If you take away anything from this section at

81

all, it should be the fact that your blog absolutely has to be mobile friendly. These days upwards of 50% of all website traffic comes from mobile devices. More and more people are increasingly using their phones to browse websites. If your blog doesn't work well on a mobile browser, then you have instantly discarded a large part of your potential audience. Thankfully, making a blog mobile friendly isn't too difficult, especially if you use the themes and plugins I recommend above.

- **Speed is Key**: Your blog needs to be fast. It isn't 1999 anymore, the advent of high-speed internet has made people lose any patience that they had for slow sites. Study after study has shown that if your website doesn't load almost instantly, then most people will close the site and never come back. Again, regardless of whether you are hiring a freelancer or designing your blog yourself, make sure that you emphasize responsiveness.

- **Simplicity is Important:** If you give your potential audience too much to click on, then they click on nothing. Your front page should feature three things prominently. A logo or title of some sort indicating what your blog does, as well as a great "*About Me*" page that lets people know who you are and why you have a blog. A featured article or article of the day that you want to use to draw people in. And finally, some sort of easy way to find previous posts or a table of contents. There is room for variation, but if you make your front page too complicated, you will pay for it down the line, so be careful.

Here Are My Top Resources Again:

Domain Names and Web Hosting: Use this link to get the insane discount on HostGator

Content Management System: Wordpress (HostGator provides this for free)

WordPress Theme: ThriveThemes (*they're my absolute favorite*)

If you have any questions, or want to hire me to help set anything up, you can email me at raza@passiveincomeplaybook.com

Chapter 6

The #1 Secret To Instantly Building Rapport W/ Your Audience

If you have been following the book's instructions step-by-step, then by now you should have quite a bit of your blog done already.

The next step involves your first bit of actual blog-related writing. No, you aren't quite at the stage of writing your first posts (but you are getting there), instead, it is time for you to create an introduction of sorts.

As I mentioned in the last chapter, you want your site to be as personable, relatable, authentic, and real as possible. That means you're going to fill out your "*About Me*" page, "*Contact Me*" page, and "*Hire Me*" page.

Remember, after your homepage, these will be the most popular pages on your blog, so you want to be very deliberate with what you include on these.

Why You Need An About Me Page

I've covered this before, but it bears repeating, a great "*About Me*" page humanizes you. It's what makes you relatable and real to the reader.

It's your *secret weapon* as a small, independent blogger.

Remember how I mentioned that people crave intimacy, authenticity, story, and emotion?

Well, this is where we're going to give it to them.

It Establishes Authority

Even though they are extremely easy to create, an "*About Me*" page still has the effect of establishing the fact that you are an authority on whatever it is that you are writing about.

When a reader reads a fully fleshed out bio, full of pictures, story, struggles, and triumphs, they'll take you a **lot** more seriously.

Your "*About Me*" page is where you state your credentials and prove that you have the solution to your readers' problems.

Even more importantly, you _**understand**_ their problems, and have the credibility, authority, and expertise to solve them.

Here's another place to list any accolades, accomplishments, awards, and social proof.

For example, my friend Ryan Robinson shows how he went from 0 to 400,000 blog readers per month.

Weight lifting blogger Mehdi of StrongLifts shares a similar story of how he went from scrawny to strong, and also documents how his blog took off.

Powerful stuff.

It Humanizes You

Years ago, I remember Steve Snell, the owner of GunDogSupply.com, say how conversions on his website jumped up after he included a picture of himself and his hunting dog.

He didn't do anything differently, just added a picture of himself and his dog.

Why did it work?

Because unlike big online retailers like Amazon, BassProShops, etc, Steve Snell was a real person that actually used the products he sold on his website.

He was a real hunter with a real hunting dog and actually used the products.

(You probably can't say the same for Jeff Bezos)

The fact that he was a real hunter, just like his customers, built instant authority, credibility, and authenticity.

So even if you're blogging to primarily make money, you don't want your blog to seem like anything more than a transparent money-making effort. People hate being sold to and they are getting much better at detecting obvious attempts to market to them.

That's why you want to spend time creating a good "*About Me*" section.

It humanizes you, it establishes a connection with your audience, and it makes your blog seem genuine. As you will see later on, putting a good story in your about me can really make your blog seem like it's run by someone who genuinely cares about what they are writing about.

It's a Great Place For Links

Finally, a more practical reason to put an "*About Me*" on your blog is that it lets you throw out some important links.

These can be links to your social media accounts, links to your "*Hire Me*" section, and any other important links that you may want to share.

Likewise, you are also going to want to include some contact info (such as an email address or two) to make it easy for someone to get in touch with you.

How to Create a Good About Me Page

My best advice is to look at the "About Me" pages of other popular blogs in your niche.

Once you do, you'll notice a common set of themes. The most popular are

- **What You Write About:** "I write about X, Y, and Z, you'll feel totally at home here."

- **Who You Write For**: Do you write for millennials? Maybe new parents? How about corporate executives? Maybe stressed out managers? Or middle-aged men that want to get back in shape. The point is you want to call out your audience specifically - it's even better if you're actually a part of your target audience. That way your readers know that you're the real deal.

- **What They'll Get:** You can tell them exactly what they'll get by reading your blog. Whether it's related to business, health, or relationships. The important thing is to make a promise of what they'll learn.

- **Where They Should Start:** This is a great place to link to your most popular content. Linking to top resources, videos, ultimate guides, and anything else that you think your readers would enjoy.

- **Your Credentials and Acknowledgements:** You can talk about where you write, like Fast Company, Entrepreneur, Forbes, etc. You can talk about how many social media followers you have. You can talk about conferences you've spoken at. You can talk about books you've written. You can talk about companies you've consulted for. You can talk about your formal education and training.

- **How You Got Started:** Every hero has an origin story. Superman came from Krypton. Batman was an orphan. Neo was a lonely computer programmer. Daniel-san was a scrawny kid. But each of them made a monumental transformation - and that's why we fell in love with them. You want to include the "hero story", including your challenges and struggles, so your readers feel connected to you too.

- **Pictures**: As a subtext to all of this, be sure to include pictures, screenshots, illustrations, videos, and documentation that verify everything you say about yourself. They further humanize you and add to your credibility.

Like I said before, a great "*About Me*" page is your secret weapon.

Now that you know how important it is and how to create one, it's time to get started.

Chapter 7

The Mind-Blowing Content Strategy To Attract Hordes Of Eager Readers

Include IncomeDiary blog post topics

All, you've made it this far, and I'm so excited for you.

Because in this chapter, we're going to get to work and start creating your content so that you can get readers.

And I'm going to share an incredibly powerful content strategy that will attract readers, build your authority, establish relationships with other influential bloggers in your niche, and become a mini-celebrity in your industry.

I'm even going to give you sample topics that you can write about so that you can hit the ground running.

Human Emotion and Ego-Bait

Everyone knows that the newspaper industry has been struggling for the past 20 years - ever since the birth of the internet.

91

Local newspapers are shutting down, large newspapers are losing ad revenue and grappling with how to remain profitable.

And yet, in a small town in the midwest of the United States, one newspaper was doing great business.

How?

Because they did stories about local businesses, personalities, politicians, and organizations. And guess what - those people that had been written about bought the newspaper!

It was a genius solution and the brilliant use of a term called ego-bait.

Ego-baiting is when you publish something flattering about someone, and then tell them about it. I'm sure you can imagine how ***powerful*** this tactic is.

So when you first start your blog, you want to create a list of the top influencers in your industry and write about them.

After you've done that, you simply send them an email with a link to your blog post and ask if they'd share it on social media.

I've tried this technique and it's incredibly powerful.

What's even better is that it's an amazing way to build relationships with influential figures in your industry. These are people that have tons of traffic that they can direct to your blog.

Once you build a relationship with these people, you can write articles on their blogs, be a guest on their podcast, and be on their videos - *all of which you can use to direct traffic to your blog.*

Top Subjects to Write About

Below, I'm going to arm you with some most powerful blog topics I can give you.

In fact, Barry Dunlop from IncomeDiary.com compiled a list of blog topics that have generated him over 1 million visitors to his blogs.

The beauty of these topics is that you can literally use them in any niche to instantly build credibility and relationships with other high authority influencers in your niche.

Why?

Because they utilize the concept of ego bait. Once he writes these articles, he emails the companies and people he's mentioned so he can slowly build a relationship with them.

The result; they share the article with their readers and invite him to write on their blog in the future.

All you have to do is fill in the blank with your industry:

- Top 30 Most Influential People In _____ (Blogging, Web Design, Photography, Golf, Gaming etc)

- 10 Reasons Why It Rocks To Be a _____ (Blogger, Web Designer, Photographer, Golfer, Gamer etc)

- 10 Reasons Why It Sucks To Be a_____ (Blogger, Web Designer, Photographer, Golfer, Gamer etc)

- 10 Christmas Gifts For _____ (Bloggers, Web Designers, Photographers, Golfers, Gamers, etc)

- 17 Tips To Cure _____ (Bloggers Block, Bad Converting Websites, Crap Photos, Golfer Elbow, Gaming Addiction, etc)

- 20 Bloggers To Follow on _____ (Facebook, Twitter, Pinterest, Google+, etc)

- Top 20 Young _____(Bloggers, Web Designers, Photographers, Golfers, Gamers, etc)

- The Top 20 _____ Who Make The Most Money (Bloggers, Web Designers, Photographers, Golfers, Gamers, etc)

- 20 Websites To Visit If You Want To Be a Better _____ (Blogger, Web Designer, Photographer, Golfer, Gamer, etc)

- 20 Best Blog Posts of 2019 For _____ (Bloggers, Web Designers, Photographers, Golfers, Gamers, etc)

These work great because they instantly allow you to arrive on the scene as an instant celebrity in your niche.

List posts are notoriously popular online and go viral quickly which is why big blogs like BuzzFeed use them to make their content go viral.

The topics above are a great start, and you can modify them and create more, but it's important that you know why they work; they use numbers, they employ ego-bait, and they're meant to be in-depth.

Be sure to write "how to" and "ultimate guide" posts that reference other influencers, bloggers, companies, and organizations in your niche.

Know Who You're Writing For

Before you start creating posts, you need to identify who your audience is. Not everyone is going to be receptive to your blog, so you need to craft your posts to appeal to those who are actually willing to sit down and read your blog.

A lot goes into figuring out who your main audience is. You have to determine things like their age, their likely occupation, what their interests are, what sorts of posts they would be interested in, etc.

Sometimes, you physically can't conceive of all this information, but that's okay because you can still craft an effective blog with just a bit of information.

Actually determining your audience involves two things, research, and a quite a few educated assumptions.

Research other blogs that cover your particular niche and see if they have posted reader surveys before, these can give you a good indication as to the gender, age range, etc. of your audience.

Another good resource is the comment section of articles pertaining to your niche. Look up an article or post that relates to your particular niche and check the comments. If the article doesn't have any helpful comments, check if it has been posted to Facebook or Twitter and if so, what are the comments like on it?

By doing this research, you can start to assemble a rough idea of what your primary blog audience is like.

As was mentioned earlier, building an audience rests a lot on educated assumptions. So, once you have some idea of what your potential audience may look like, you can start to think about what their interests are and why they might browse your blog.

For example, let's say you are running a cooking blog and you have determined that your primary audience is women in their 30s and 40s. Now, you can ask yourself the very important question, "what would they be browsing my blog for?" This is where you have to make educated assumptions.

Women at that age are likely to have families, so they could be browsing your blog for new, healthy recipes to try and get their kids to eat healthier. They're also likely to be looking for new recipes in general, either to spice up family dinners or to impress friends. Finally, you can also assume that they have some level of disposable income, and so they may be looking for reviews of products.

The purpose of gathering this information is to determine what types of posts will do well on your blog. While the example above was focused on cooking, you can do that sort of thing for any niche, whether it be finance, cars, etc.

Creating a Content Calendar

Professionals of all kinds, from athletes, to scientists, to astronauts, to writers, to salespeople know the importance of "logging hours" - in other words, the importance to sitting down and spending the time to get work done.

Now that you've got some awesome topics to write about, you need to come up with a content calendar where you schedule your blog posts and when you write and publish them.

Having a content calendar ensures that your blog is updated regularly. This builds trust with readers and with search engines because your blog is relevant, up to date, and recent.

Now that you have a list of topics, you don't have to worry about writer's block.

Instead of having to sit down and say "Alright, what am I going to write about today," you can sit down and say "Alright, today I am scheduled to write about x." It really does make your life a lot easier.

Typically, good bloggers will plan out at least a month's worth of content. If you want, you can, of course, plan out a lot more.

Developing a content strategy is a non-negotiable step when it comes to blogging. While you can certainly blog without one, you are just making your life a lot more difficult for no real reason. You will spend a lot more time writing posts and your posts won't get as much traction. So, there is no real reason not to create one.

Key Takeaways:

We went through a lot in this chapter.

- Top subjects to write about

- Know your audience

- Create a content calendar

Remember to make your content personable, relatable, and authentic because that's what people crave.

Chapter 8

How To Create Mind-Blowingly Good Blog Posts
(*They'll Go Viral And Generate Massive Traffic*)

In this chapter, it is time to finally tackle one of the most important aspects of blogging, actually writing your blog posts.

If you go back a few chapters, you will find a discussion of the various places to host your blog. That chapter recommended using WordPress. Now, this book can't possibly account for every option, so it will be written primarily with the idea of WordPress in mind. Almost all of the tips related to writing will apply to any platform, but this section, in particular, will be discussing how to actually publish a post and thus will be relevant mostly to those using WordPress. If you aren't using WordPress, you might want to skip to the next section.

Publishing a blog post when using WordPress is extremely easy. Simply go to the "posts" section and click "add new." From there you will see a bunch of boxes to be filled. Technically, all you need to fill in is the boxes marked "title" and "post." But you may also want to familiarize yourself with things like adding images and links, as you will want to do those quite a bit when writing as well.

It is a good idea to familiarize yourself with how to actually go about uploading a blog post before you start writing one as it will make your life a lot easier down the road. However, you should write your blog post directly into WordPress (despite you being able to write your entire blog post in WordPress in theory). WordPress's writing system is very clunky and shouldn't be used for more than small changes. Instead, write your post in Microsoft Word and then just copy and paste it into WordPress.

What to Include in Every Blog Post

Writing is a skill, and the more you do it, the better you'll get. Luckily, you don't have to worry about writer's block because you have a list of amazing topics to write about and a content calendar where you've pre-scheduled when you're going to write and publish.

So writing should be straight-forward. You may not like the quality of your writing at first, but remember, you'll get better with practice. Also remember that most popular writers, bloggers, and authors are embarrassed by their early work - but they kept going anyway.

Since you already have a list of topics to write about, I'm going to share what you need to include in every blog post.

These tips are used by the most popular web writers in the world.

And make no mistake, there's a big difference between writing novels and writing for the web.

Online, your content needs to be focused on selling, that means you need to write amazing headlines and make the content scannable and easy to read.

Here's a high-level list of what you need to include in every blog post you write:

- *An awesome headline*

- *Captivating images*

- *Short sentences, subheadings, and bullet points*

- *Story*

- *Tons of links to other articles, blog posts, and resources in your niche*

- *At least 2000 words in the format of list posts/How-to Guides/Ultimate Guides*

- *A clear call to action*

We'll cover each one of these in detail below.

Use Strong Headlines

Your headline is that will attract people to your blog post.

Like I said before, top copywriters spend 80% of their time coming up with a perfect headline because they know how impactful it is.

There tons of headline formulas, but successful one's are:

- Top X Ways to Do _____ Without _____

- The Ultimate Guide to _____ (with pictures)

- 45 Shocking Reasons to _____

- The #1 Secret to _____ in 30 Days

- How _____ Can Do _____ Without Having
  to _____

- WARNING: This is the REAL Reason You Can't
  _____

- Double Your _____ Results in the Next 90 Days

- The ____ Top Websites/Blogs in _____ for 2019

These headlines create curiosity, imply a benefit, and hit at a solution to a problem.

I'm sure you can see how powerful they are just by taking a look at them.

Use Lots of Captivating Images

Every blog post you write should include a featured image. The featured image is the image that will appear on the homepage of your blog. Along with your headline, it should really convince the reader to click on the article and read it.

As I said earlier, you want to include as many images, screenshots, videos, diagrams, and illustrations as you can to prove your point and establish your legitimacy and credibility.

You know, a picture is worth 1000 words.

Images have two primary functions on a blog. Firstly, they help to make your content a lot more appealing to the eye. When writing text-heavy posts, including images at regular intervals can be really helpful. Not only will they catch the eye of your reader, but they also act like subheadings in that they can help break up large blocks of text.

Secondly, images are good because people will often share them on social media, with the link leading back to your blog. So, making good use of images can often be a free form of advertising (and a very effective one at that).

You don't have to take pictures yourself. With the internet, you have access to an endless source of free images. It doesn't matter what sorts of images that you need, you can find them for free on the internet, just don't steal anyone else's images or you might have some problems.

Two great sites for free images are:

- Pixabay.com

- Unsplash.com

Use Short Sentences, Subheadings, Bold, Italics, Underlines, and Bullet Points

Always remember, you're writing for an online audience with short attention spans and a wealth of information at their fingertips.

That's why it's so important you make your blog posts scannable, easy to read, and actionable - otherwise, your readers will simply click off and go somewhere else.

There are a few things you can do to make your posts more readable including writing in short sentences, using subheadings, and bullet points.

In fact, some of the greatest English writers, including Ernest Hemingway, were fond of writing short sentences. Writing short, punchy, powerful sentences drives your point home the same way as if you were having a conversation with a friend.

Unless you're a really good writer, long, comma-filled sentences will add fluff to your writing and confuse the reader. So focus on brevity and conciseness.

In addition to writing short sentences, you want to write short paragraphs - they should be 2 to 3 sentences each.

You'll notice that some of the world's most popular blogs employ this strategy… and you should too.

To further make your blog posts easier to read, include lots of subheadings. Subheadings allow readers to quickly scan your content. That makes it easier for them to retain information because they're getting a quick preview of the topic before digging in. Creating subheadings also serve as a frame of reference, making it easier to read and remember the content.

To make it even easier to read and remember, you want to include lots of bullet points. This will make it easier to hone in on the key points that you want your readers to remember. It also makes it easier to read your content.

Lastly, use bold, italics, and underlines to emphasize your points.

Tell Your Story

The only thing that separates your content from the millions of other bloggers out there is your story.

You can write the best, most technically sound blog post in the world, but if it's sterile and devoid of story, it'll fall flat on its face.

Humans love drama, emotion, story, imagery, personality, and suspense, so your writing has to deliver that.

Even if your writing is mediocre, readers will forgive you as long as you include story and emotion. It can be your own story of struggle, heartbreak, difficulty, and eventual triumph. Or it can be someone else's.

The point is that you have to tell your story and speak from the heart because that's what will get your audience to emotionally connect with you.

That's why we love The Karate Kid, Terminator, The Last Samurai, The Matrix, The Notebook, etc. The emotion, story, and ups and downs that the characters went through is captivating.

Even if you're doing an instructional blog post, write it in a personal tone as it is simply more engaging. Don't just tell someone that something works, tell them why it has worked for you. Don't just say "this rice cooker can cook five different kinds of rice." Instead, say "I've been able to use this rice cooker to cook five delicious kinds of rice." It is a small change, but it makes your writing a lot more engaging.

Share your story every chance you get.

Write Long Content

When I saw long content, I mean each blog post should be at least 2000 words. In fact, my friend and top blogger Ryan Robinson writes blog posts that are 4000-5000 words!

It sounds like a lot of work, but if you're interested in really helping your readers, this is a no brainer.

Why?

Because you want to write the best content you possibly can for your readers. That means you need to really dig deep and write something that will truly change their lives.

This is how you differentiate yourself from the thousands of other bloggers writing about the same topic as you. This is how you connect with your readers. This is how you show other people in your industry that you're serious about what you do. This is how you show search engines like Google that you're a credible, authoritative site.

It takes work, but the end results are EPIC.

The superiority of longer content has been known for a while and SEO experts have been telling people for a long time to make longer content a key part of their website building strategy.

Many people still ignore it because writing unique, long content is difficult. If you want proof, look no further than Neil Patel, a British online marketer with a lot of experience. He conducted an analysis of over 20,000 keywords on Google.

What he found was that the top 10 search results for each keyword all had one thing in common, long content (more specifically, content that is over 2000 words long). The evidence is all there, long content simply ranks better.

The best kind of content is list posts, ultimate guides, and how to posts similar to the headlines that I shared earlier in this chapter.

If you used the tips I mentioned above (images, subheadings, short sentences, bullet points, etc.), your content will be easy to read and your readers will love you for it.

Mention Others Often

I mentioned ego-bait in the last chapter, and I want you to take that idea to heart.

Remember, when you're starting out you won't have many connections or much of a follower base.

The easiest way to grow both is to mention *others*.

I know it sounds counterintuitive to refer your readers to other sites, but it works amazingly well for a few different reasons.

First, when you link to other blogs, articles, organizations, and people in your industry, you can easily email them and tell them that they've made a huge impact on you so you mentioned them in your article. You can then ask them to share your article with their followers. This is an amazing way to get traffic to your content because these influencers likely have huge followings. It's also a great way to build a relationship with them so that you can write on their blog or appear on their podcast.

Secondly, mentioning others builds trust with your readers. Imagine going to a party and recommending people to your favorite barber, or referring people to your favorite babysitter, or telling people about an awesome restaurant you went to. Over time, they'll start to value your opinion and view you as an authority. They'll know that you aren't talking about yourself - instead, you're talking about others, which shows that you're "in the know".

Lastly, search engines reward you for linking out to other high authority sites. You'll be seen as a trusted part of the ecosystem and Google will start to trust you and rank you highly in their search engine - leading to natural traffic to your blog.

A Clear Call to Action

Every single blog post should end with a call to action.

99% of the time it should be to sign up for your email newsletter. Since you're investing so much time in creating great content, you want your readers to become followers - and the best way to do that is for them to join your email newsletter.

After they're on your newsletter, you can email them about new content, products and services, or even ask them for feedback on future blog posts.

In rare cases, you can include a call to action to buy something, but inviting them to join your email newsletter is non-negotiable because you need to build a following.

Proper Keyword Usage

By far the most important SEO tool at your disposal are keywords. Keywords are phrases that Google uses to help people find content. For example, "best rice cooker" would be considered a keyword. People type that phrase into Google and Google looks for sites with that keyword.

If you want people to find your content more easily on Google, then you need to be conscious of what keywords you are using. Google offers a free keyword tool that tells you how many people are typing a certain phrase into Google monthly.

Before writing a blog post, type a few relevant phrases into the keyword tool and see how many people are typing those phrases monthly. If the number is decent (a couple thousand), then you might want to use those phrases in your blog post.

For example, let's say I'm doing a blog post on the best rice cookers on Amazon. Some of the phrases I might consider using would be "best rice cookers," "best rice cooker," "best rice cookers under $500," "best budget rice cooker."

By sprinkling these phrases throughout my blog post, I can make my blog appear higher on Google whenever someone searches for these phrases or phrases that are closely related.

Keywords are like a fine spice. When they are used well, they can help boost a post. However, when they are used poorly (either by not using enough or by using too many), then they either have no effect or they ruin the post.

When using keywords, you should always have a primary keyword. This keyword will appear in your title, your introduction, the middle of your article, and at the end of your post. You can also have secondary keywords that get sprinkled throughout the rest of the blog post.

You should aim for a keyword density (the number of times your keywords appear in the post) of around 1%. What this means is that if you are writing a 1500-word blog post, you should use your keywords around 15 times throughout the entire post.

Avoid keyword spamming (using a keyword an excessive number of times), as this will result in Google penalizing your blog or straight up banning it from appearing on its search results.

Finally, when deciding which keywords to use, keep the number of searches in mind. Keywords with higher search numbers are likely to be heavily contested. When your blog is just starting out, it might be smarter to target keywords with a smaller number of searches (a couple of thousand) as many other blogs will overlook these keywords when making their own posts.

Key TakeAways

I covered a lot in this chapter, and if you follow this advice, every blog post will be a winner.

Just take it seriously and be sure to include the following in every blog post:

- *An awesome headline*

- *Captivating images*

- *Short sentences, subheadings, and bullet points*

- *Story*

- *Tons of links to other articles, blog posts, and resources in your niche*

- *At least 2000 words in the format of list posts/How-to Guides/Ultimate Guides*

- *A clear call to action*

- *Proper use of keywords*

Chapter 9

The Step-By-Step To Get Featured On The Biggest Blogs, Podcasts, And Websites In Your Industry
(And Send A Stampede Of Visitors To Your Blog)

In the last chapter I covered how to create amazing blogs posts.

In this chapter I'm going to go over how to promote them.

I know this sounds crazy, but you want to spend just as much time promoting your content as you do writing it - which is why it's **_so_** critically important to create amazing blog posts that reference other people.

By writing amazing blog posts, your dramatically increasing the chances that you'll get massive traffic - after all, you've got to have a high-quality product before you spend time promoting it.

Once you've got amazing content, promoting it is much easier.

In fact, Barry Dunlop of IncomeDiary.com often writes dozens of blog posts, and publishes them at once. Posting a large number of articles (10 - 20) instantly builds credibility for your blog because it's got tons of content already.

That makes outreach to other bloggers much easier because your blog already looks established.

It would look silly to spend a bunch of time marketing your blog, only for readers to visit and find only one or two posts for them to read.

So, have at least a couple, sizeable posts for potential visitors to actually read before you start doing serious marketing.

The Power of Other People's Audience

Throughout this book, I've mentioned the concept of ego-bait, and for good reason. If you can build authentic, real relationships with influencers in your industry, they'll give you access to their audience.

In fact, some of the world's most popular bloggers became famous because someone bigger than them gave them access to their audience.

For example, Leo Babauta of ZenHabits.net wrote dozens of guest posts, which cemented his status as one of the most prolific and influential bloggers on the planet.

NerdFitness.com owner Steve Kamb became famous because he built a relationship with mega-successful podcaster John Lee Dumas.

Business is about relationships, and no one becomes a success without the help of others. So pay a lot of attention to building strong relationships with others in your industry.

The Secret Method to Build Relationships with Influencers in Your Niche

In this section, I'm going to outline a simple strategy you can use to connect and build relationships with other influential people in your industry.

It's called influencer outreach, and in this section, I'm going to show you exactly how I've built relationships with influential bloggers in my niche.

The key is to be authentic. No one wants to work with someone that's only worried about themselves. If you show genuine concern and interest in others, they'll gladly help you.

I've paid hundreds of dollars to learn the steps I share below.

In addition to that, I've used them myself to connect with influential people in my industry, and I've seen others do the exact same thing over and over again.

So take this seriously because *it works*.

How to Build Relationships w/ Influencers

1) Create a list of the top 50 blogs, websites, publications, forums, podcasts, YouTube videos, Facebook groups, Medium publications, in your industry. You can simply perform a Google search to create your list.

2) Create a spreadsheet that documents the following information:

   • Name

- Email address

- Contact page

- Topic/Niche

- Type (blog, podcast, Facebook group, etc.)

- Twitter name

- Previous positive outreach

- Previous negative outreach

- Notes

- Segment

- Correspondence status

- Confirmed interest?

- Promotional dates locked down?

- List size

- Click through rate

- Next steps

3)   You need to get on their radar by interacting with their content for at least two weeks. Here are some of the best ways to do it:

- Join their email newsletter and reply to them

- Leave deep, thoughtful comments on their blog posts

- Leave an authentic review of their podcast

- Comment in their Facebook group

- Like, comment, and share a recent Twitter post of theirs (and then tag them)

- Send them a personal email mentioning that you added them to a blog post about top bloggers. Or tell them something that you specifically learned **and** applied from them (they'll love this because you're showing them how they made an impact on you)

Remember: do not ask them for anything when you contact them. You're a complete stranger to them and there's no reason why they would be willing to help you. You have to first build a relationship with them, and then, when the time is right, ask them for help.

4)   Do everything I mentioned above for at least 2 weeks. Be sure **not** to mention your blog or ask for anything. The goal is to be authentic, genuine, and helpful so that you get on their radar.

The only exception to this rule is if you mention that you wrote about them.

5)   Offer to help them with something. You can send an email that says something like:

"I love your work (as you can probably tell from all of the comments and retweets I've been leaving on your blog!)

Anyway, I was wondering how I can help you. You've helped me a lot because _____ and I want to return the favor

Raza

P.S.

I've been working on a really special way to get _____ results. I think it would really help your audience and I'd love to tell you about it."

Believe me when I tell you; this strategy works.

Once you've built a relationship with someone, you can use it to be interviewed on their podcast or write a guest post on their blog.

I've used this strategy to get featured by marketer and blogger Guy Kawasaki and to write guest posts for large, influential bloggers.

Other Ways to Get Traffic to Your Blog

The method I outlined above will help you build relationships with influential people in your market. And those relationships will turn into traffic to your website.

But there are a handful of other ways to get traffic as well. What you'll notice, is that all of these methods leverage the built-in popularity of these platforms. So rather than struggling to get traffic, you're getting traffic directly from websites that already have hundreds of millions of visitors.

1)   Re-post on Medium and LinkedIn:

Whenever you write a blog post, copy and paste it on something like Medium and LinkedIn.

2)   Create a YouTube Video of Every Blog Post:

The easiest way is to use the camera on your computer or phone and just talk about what you just wrote about.

Don't worry if your videos aren't that great in the beginning. They'll get better.

3) Promote on Quuu:

Quuu is a website where people pay to promote their content on social media. It costs about $40 for a one-month promotion, but it'll get social media traffic to your blog posts. If your post is good, it'll also get organic traffic.

4) Build an Email List:

This is absolutely non-negotiable. It's so important that I'm going to write about it in the next chapter.

Key Takeaways:

There are hundreds of ways to generate traffic to your blog, but I wanted to show you the simplest, most effective, easiest ways to do that.

And that comes down to building relationships with other more influential people in your niche.

You also want to build a presence on large sites like YouTube, Medium, LinkedIn, and use tools like Quuu to get lots of social shares.

Lastly, you want to focus on email marketing to build your audience.

Chapter 10

Email Marketing Magic

This will be a short chapter, but it's absolutely **_vital_** to your success as a blogger.

I ignored it for the longest amount of time, and I really regret it.

Social media followers are fickle. They may follow you, but they won't do very much else.

Social media platforms are even worse, they may bring you traffic one day, and then change their algorithms and you'll lose your effectiveness.

This happened when Facebook decided to decrease the organic reach of Facebook pages. Facebook pages that spent time and effort to build hundreds of thousands of followers were suddenly unable to communicate with their users unless they paid. Visibility on organic posts dropped to single-digit percentages.

That's why the best way to promote your content is to have your own follower base on a platform that you own.

That platform is your email list.

Remember how important relationships with big influencers are? The same goes for your audience

Once you have an email list, you can ask them for feedback, promote special offers, and rely on them to be your most ardent supporters.

Every time you release a new blog post, you can email them and let them know.

I've personally launched my books, my courses, and my coaching programs to my email list - to the tune of thousands of dollars.

So please don't underestimate building an email list.

And every single visitor on your blog should be able to quickly and easily join your email list.

All you have to do is have a popup on your site and offer a free report, cheatsheet, checklist, or exclusive video.

Some of the biggest bloggers in the world from Brian Clark, to Ryan Robinson, to Neil Patel, to Barry Dunlop all use their email list to grow their audience and sales.

I personally recommend **GetResponse** to build your email list. I've been using them for years and they have great features and pricing.

I've got nearly 10,000 email subscribers and my #1 goal is to not only grow my email list, but to build a deeper relationship with them.

You should do the same.

Key TakeAways:

This is a short chapter for a reason - email marketing works and is an absolute necessity.

I personally recommend GetResponse because they have great prices, useful features, and amazing customer support. I chat with their support technicians all the time and they're incredibly responsive.

Click here to get started with **GetResponse** - you can even get started for free.

If you have any questions, or want to hire me to help set it up, you can email me at

raza@passiveincomeplaybook.com

Chapter 11

The BEST Way To Make Money From Your Blog

I'm really excited for you because you've come a long way.

By now you have selected a topic to blog about, you've bought a catchy domain name and hosting, you've installed Wordpress, you've uploaded a Wordpress theme, you've come up with a list of topics to write about, you've set up your email software, and are starting to interact with other influencers in your industry.

(If not, then get started, it's much easier than you think)

Now we talk about making money from your blog.

At the beginning of this book, I mentioned a lot of great methods. Things like:

- Coaching

- Consulting

- Online courses

- Affiliate marketing

- Paid speaking

- Advertising

- Paid/Sponsored product reviews

And they're all viable ways to make money from your blog.

But I want to give you the quickest, easiest, simplest way to make money.

But before I do, I want to tell you a story.

About 15 years ago, I started a blog about offshore software outsourcing. I saw that lots of offshore projects failed because they were basically software sweatshops, so I decided to create a blog called SoftwareSweatshop.com

A few months after starting my blog, a customer from Belgium contacted me for a software project.

I did no other marketing besides writing a few blog posts - and that turned into a $2000/month client.

I was shocked.

But it works like a charm.

So, the simplest, easiest, fastest way to start earning six-figures from your blog is to offer a service.

The formula is simple:

Write amazing blog posts that discuss relevant problems in your industry → Talk about how to solve those problems → Have a "Hire Me" link in the navigation of your website

Easy.

And the fact that you're writing amazing blog posts with images, great headlines, bullet points, subheadings, and transformational stories will build trust and intimacy with your audience like nothing else.

Blogging makes you an authority in your industry and will cause people to contact you to help them.

Sure, it's very possible to make money from affiliate marketing, or courses, or speaking, but it takes a long time.

Offering your coaching, consulting, or some other type of service is the ***best*** way to quickly and easily make money from your blog.

My friend Ryan Robinson blogs about online marketing and charges $5,000 per month to do content marketing for companies. And they all find him because of his blog.

Tons of other bloggers do the same thing.

Whether you offer personal finance services, or photography, or editing, or sales consulting, or marriage counseling, or personal training, or software development, or online marketing, you have valuable skills that people are willing to pay for.

You just have to position yourself as an expert by writing amazing blog posts and showing them how you solve their problems.

You Can Do It

Throughout this book, I shared a TON of great tips and strategies for making a successful blog.

If you follow what this book says, and if you are willing to put in the work, then you are well on your way to having an extremely successful blog.

While blogging isn't going to give you a fortune overnight, it can definitely pay off well in the end.

Below I've collected my list of top resources and my contact information if you want to hire me to set anything up for you.

Recommended Resources

Here are my *absolute favorite* resources. I personally use them and can't recommend them enough.

I make a commission if you buy any of these products, but I would recommend them even if I didn't - plus, you're getting a massive discount on these tools.

They'll make your life easier and help you get your blog started in a matter of days.

1). Domain Names and Web Hosting: HostGator

They have incredible customer service and make setting up a blog a breeze.

Click here for my special discount bundle offer for $3/month.

2). Wordpress Theme: ThriveThemes

They are the best Wordpress theme I've ever seen. They have amazing features for an incredibly low price:

- Beautiful landing page builders

- A drag-and-drop website builder

- Gorgeous templates

- Viral quizzes

Click here to watch their video and sign up

3). Email Marketing Service: GetResponse

I've used them for years and their customer service is stellar.

Click here to get 30 days for free.

4). The BEST Blogging Course on the Market: Built to Blog

If you're interested in the BEST course on the market about blogging, you've got to check out Built to Blog by Ryan Robinson.

He gets over 10,000 visitors to his blog per day, and is currently making $50,000 per month from his blog (*you read that right*)

His course is amazing and he shows you how he earned $100,000 from his blog in less than a year by working 10-15 hours per week and how to scale it up to $50k per month.

Click here to get his course

Lastly, if you have any questions, or want to hire me to help set anything up, you can email me at raza@passiveincomeplaybook.com

Before You Leave A Review…

Thank you again for buying and reading this book. If you got this far, it's because you finished the book, so congratulations!

Authors live and die by the reviews we receive from our readers. So if you liked this book, I'd really appreciate if you left it a 5-star review.

If you didn't like this book, <u>before you leave a negative review</u>, please email me at <u>raza@passiveincomeplaybook.com</u> and let me know what you would like me to improve. The beauty of publishing online is that I can instantly add content, fix errors, and update information.

So if there's something you didn't like, or that you'd like me to remove, please email me so I can fix it.

Thanks!